I dedicate this book to those
who have never met
my Friend.

Special thanks to:

- Jordan Whitmer
  Who's simple testimony inspired this writing
- Sarah Barlow
  Cover design
- Janet Peluso
  Editorial and layout guidance
- Tim Aikenhead
  Editorial guidance
- Joseph Barlow Ministries Partners
  For sending me to do the work

Scripture quotes are taken from:

- The New Living Translation
  Tyndale House Publishers, 1996 Carol Stream, IL

ISBN: 978-0-9971678-7-0

Texting Through the Clouds

Your Quest

by

Joseph Barlow

A Publication of
Joseph Barlow Ministries
www.josephbarlow.com

Texting Through the Clouds
Your Quest

by Joseph Barlow

Introduction

As a little boy, I used to listen in on my parent's and elder siblings' conversations. I learned so much from that vantage point. Later, entering into the conversations, I was well-prepared. Today, you will read a conversation but maybe it will become your own.

In many places in this book, I've placed very few words on a page, that is intentional. Take the thought, digest it. You'll see, it really is a page-worth of thinking.

Enjoy!

Joe

Your Beginning…

You were
created…

You were
created by God.

You weren't just birthed into this world.

God sent you
here.

You are on a
quest.

You have a
Quest,

it's wrapped up
inside of you,

but it is written.

We all have a Quest.

Some never discover it.

But it's there in each of us waiting to be unwrapped.

Have you found yours?

Opposition is real.
It's there to contend.
Or tempt you to join them,
please don't befriend.

Subtle and swaying,
distracting, destructing;

anything

to keep your attention from
discovering the Quest that
dwells deep inside you.

You

are the answer to this difficult world.

For this day

and

for this time,

you

were chosen.

You were sent.

The answer
is in you.

It's part of Your Quest.

You must now
discover it.

Sent!

Sent for a reason.

Sent for this season.

A Curious Text…

Hey?

?

You don't know me,
but I know you.

I've known about you
longer than you've
been alive!

I've been hoping for
a chance to talk with
you.

I know your family
and friends.

I may have some
insight for you.

Can we talk?

Sure.

The family was
supposed to be there
for you, right?

How'd that
get blown up
before I even
arrived?

A cocoon of love
and nurture and help,
but not everyone got
that…

…crippled at
best.

Some had attacks,
beatings, abuse, the
system was broken,
like stuck in a noose.

Completely in pain.
Completely
distracted.

There was another plan you're saying?

The poverty, the lack, the loneliness was awful.

Darkness was everywhere, how was I supposed to avoid it?

What are you saying?

Is there a higher life?

I see some floating with ease.

They don't have to deal with this life of disease.

Should I just hate them?

They anger me so.

I can't stand that they have what
I've wanted so badly.

Jealousy and hatred
I've entered in gladly.

The ones that you envy have pain of
their own.

If you knew its depth,
you'd gladly retreat to your own.

Joys and pains are on
everyone's plate.

But mine hurt!

I know.

I'm sorry that it hurts beyond
what it seems you can bear.

I'm sorry that there hasn't been
someone there.

Someone to lean on.

Someone to trust.

Someone to listen.

Someone to care.

Here's a clue to Your Quest:

I don't want others to
feel as much pain as you have.

I want you to help them.

Who are you?

I created you.

You're
real?

I Am!

Where have
you been?

I've been here.

Waiting for you.

Watching.

Wanting in.

Waiting.

Why did you
wait?

You had to open the
door for me.

?

I am here.

What do you
want?

You!

Really?

Can you sense this
becoming real?

                              Not sure…

I am real.

Can you feel me
drawing you?

                              I am drawn.
                    Do you really want me?

                    Haven't you seen
                    what I've done?

                    Haven't you heard
                    my thoughts?
              Don't you know the real me?

Yes.
I want you.
I've chosen you.

I know the real you.

But you have never
really met the real
you.

Interesting.

I'll show you.

What do I do?

Call me.

huh?

(silence)

I don't get it…

Call my name.

I'll answer.

What is your name?

I Am Jesus.

The Son of God.

I was sent to save you.

Save me?

From what?

(silence)

You know…

I guess I know.

You don't know the
half of it.

There's so much
more,

but I'm still saving
you from it.

You mean there's more
pain and suffering ahead?

There was and is.

But I'm saving you
from the ultimate
suffering.

You mean
there's worse
than what I've
endured?

Way!

Wow.

(silence)

?

Call me.

Your name?

Yes.

Call me!

If you call on my
name,

I answer you!

I cleanse you!

I forgive you!

I give you strength.

I will give you more
than strength.

I will give you power
to bring forth
Your Quest.

My Quest?

I sent you into this
earth with a mission,
a quest.

It's wrapped up
inside of you.

I want to help you
unwrap it…

to become it…

to complete it.

This is where you
find your sense of
fulfillment.

Becoming fully…
you!

You are who I've
created you to be.

But, like I said,
you've never fully met
yourself.

I knew what I was doing
when I made you.

I will show you
what I've placed
inside of you

You will be surprised.

You'll actually be
delighted.

Things that
you've wondered
about yourself…

Things that
you didn't understand…

I'll show you the real you.

Some
of what you think you are
isn't the real you.

There's been
much confusion,

but if you'll listen,

I'll explain it all.

I'm willing to teach you.

I love you.

                                                        ?

(silence)

                                                        ?

I do.

Call Me…

Call me.

                    Right now?

(smile) (nod)

                    Out loud?

(BIGGER smile)

                    Are you sure
                    you want me?
                    I'm getting to
                    the point of
                    really wanting
                    you,
                    but are you
                    sure?

                    Me?

Call me.

Don't be afraid.

OK

(whisper)
Jesus?

Yes!

Be bold.

A little louder.

Jesus!

Yes!

Call me like you need
me.

Like you need my
help.

Jesus!

Are you willing to let
me be God?

But you are
God!

Yes, but in your life,
are you willing to let
me?

Sure.

Are you willing to put
me in that position in
your life?

As Lord?

Yes!

Call me again with
that in mind.

Jesus.

Lord Jesus!

You are mine, child.
And I Am yours.
Forever!

I'm so happy about
this.

So am I!

I have more for you.

Really?

A lot more.

Like what?

Let's talk.

Okay.

You know all those
things you did that

you know were
wrong?

                                        Yes.

I forgive you.

                                   Really?

All of it.
It's all washed away.

Your record is clean.

You can let go of all
that past stuff.

                                   Really?

That feels
great.

Really?

All of it?

Complete!

Thank you.

I have something I
want you to do.

Well, you are
my Lord now,
so go for it.

Remember all those things that other people did to you that hurt you?

You know they knew what they were doing? Right?

But they still did it.

Some of them didn't know what they were doing.

But they hurt you.

I want you to forgive them.

Just like
you forgave
me?

(smile) (nod)

Some of
those people
really hurt
me.

I know.

I was there.

I saw the whole
thing.

How?

Actually,
just so you know,

you didn't see the whole thing.

I saw every spirit that was active in those situations.

All you saw were the ones hurting you.

There were more players active in those situations.

The people hurting you didn't really know about those other spirits that were at work there.

Those people were just filled with hate or anger. They were filled with wicked thoughts.

But those thoughts
were fed into them.

They really didn't
know what they were
doing.

Think of it this way,
some people, when they
watch a puppet show
get mad at the puppets.

The evil spirits you
couldn't see were acting
like puppet masters.

The people hurting you
were just like the puppets.

They didn't know they
were being manipulated.

Forgive them child.

I want you
to let them go free.

I've taken away
your sins.

Release them from theirs.

Your heart is free
from vengeance toward them.

Let them go.

Forgive them.

I let them go.

Lord, I forgive them.

How does that feel?

Well, I'm not excited
about them getting
off totally free.

But…

But that's what I'm
doing for you.

                              Yes.

Are you letting them go?

                              Yes.

Are you sure?

                              Yes.

Thank you for doing that.

When you forgive them,
you think you just
set them free,
but really,
you just set yourself
free!

Since I Am God
and you're not,
you can let me be
the judge of them.

Being their judge
is too heavy of a weight
for you.

That was a big deal.

I know.

My Book…

Keeping your heart
free is going to be
key to this life with
me.

What do you
mean?

People's hearts get
all tangled up in lots
of things. There's so
much that can throw
you off.

I'll teach you how to
operate from a place
of peace.

When I walked the
earth that's how I did
it. From a place of
total peace.

There was no war
going on inside me.

When you walked the earth?

You haven't read my book.

Are you an author?

It was written about me.

Have you heard of the Bible?

Yes.
Is that a book?

Yes, it's a bunch of books all rolled into one.

It's about me.

I want you to read it.
You'll get to know a
lot more about me.
You'll get to know me
better.

But you'll need help
reading it.

I'll give you my Holy
Spirit to be with you
and guide you into
the truth.

Some people have
read my book and
interpreted it in
different ways. But
they don't all know
me.

But if you learn from
my Holy Spirit,
He never gets it
wrong.

I'm excited to
learn.

I'll send you teachers
to guide you as well.

My Spirit will guide
you about who to
listen to.

Many teach from my
book, but again, they
don't all know me.

I have those who
have heard my voice
and have been
taught by my Spirit.
Their words are like
fire.

They will kindle your
heart. Stay close to
me and you'll know if
they're right.

I want you to know
my book…

I have placed the
road map to the
fulfillment of
Your Quest in those
pages. But just like a
good mystery you
must seek out all the
clues. My Holy Spirit
will coach you
through the whole
process.

Also, it'll take you a
lifetime to find and
fulfill Your Quest.

But it'll be worth it.

I guarantee.

My Power…

Power!

Huh?

Power!

?

You need power.

Yeah?

I have a weird
question for you.

Okay.

What if I made you
to be a sugar cone?

You mean like
an ice cream
cone?

Without the ice cream.

Just the cone?

Yeah.

Why would you do that?

Why would I
want to live my life
without the ice cream?

Why would I just want
to be the sugar cone?

That's what I want to
know!?

I don't get it?

I make you the
sugar cone,

then,

when you ask,

I fill you with the sweetest,

best tasting ice cream

anyone has ever had.

It's like the sugar cone
meets its destiny when
it's filled with ice cream
and served up.

Truth!

haha

The world is starving
for my Spirit.

Like ice cream,
I want to…

serve Him…

to the world…

but, in you.

I'll be a cone!

Are you willing?

Will you fill
me?

Remember all the
pain?

That we
talked about
before?

Yes.

Without you,

there are so many
who will never stop
feeling that pain.

Your Quest
is a rescue mission.

But I had to transform
you first.

You had to call me,

receive me,

hear me,

know me,

let go of wrong identities.

You had to let me
work on the inside,
sorting everything out.

As I fill you with my Spirit
and serve you to
the world,
everything changes.

This is the power.

This is your mission.

Your Quest!

Do **you** want it?

Definitely!

Then ask me.

?

Just ask.

My Holy Spirit has
already been poured
out into the earth.

He's already here,
but He can't do His
work in you fully until
you ask me.

How do I do
it?

Just say,
"Lord, fill me with
your Holy Spirit,
the power to live this
life, the power to
fulfill my purpose.
The same power
You lived this life
with."

Okay…

Lord, fill me…

Done!

What?

Done!

Uh! Uh, I don't know what to say.

I know.
Say it anyway.
Let me speak through you.
You don't have to understand it.

What is this?

It's Me.

Go ahead.

Let it flow.

Sounds crazy
doesn't it.

It's me.

Am I okay?

More than okay.

Your tongue is
where a huge
amount of this power
will flow.

Yes, I'll use your
hands and your
hugs, your eyes, and
your smile,
but I have to be able
to speak through
your mouth.

This is amazing. I've never felt anything like this. Yet, it feels so normal.

Let it flow.

Now call my name.

Jesus!

Yes!

Praise you Jesus!

You really are
God!

You really are
good!

Your Life...

Can we keep talking?

Sure!

You know you're
talking to someone
who is invisible,
right?

But you've
made
yourself so
real to me.

I know you.

Yes, you do.

I am here.

I Am!

You know you're my
child now,
right?

Yes.

I have other children
I want you to meet.

That's great.

You'll love being a
part of the family.

It's my family.

I'm glad you've
joined us.

Thanks.

I'll introduce you,
but I have a simple
rule in my family.

You ready?

Sure.

This is big.

        Okay…

Love!

        No problem.

Great!
I like your attitude.
But there are times it
won't be so easy.

That's why I've made
love to be a
supernatural force
and I've placed it on
the inside of you.

There are some
people who aren't so
loveable.

Really because
they're empty.
No one ever filled
them with love.

But you,
I'm expecting a lot
from you. Because
you know me.

(smile)

You know that I love
you right?

I definitely
can feel it.
It's very real.

Stay in that love.
I want you to
experience that for
the rest of your life.

Oh, that's
right, I'm
going to die
someday.

Yes, but now you
don't have to worry
about that day.

But
everybody's
afraid of
death.

You don't have to be
anymore.

It's like a door.
I'll be waiting just on
the other side.

I'll always be with
you here.

But I'll be there
waiting.

(silence)

I'm so glad I
met you.

Now don't plan on
being done anytime
soon.

Don't forget Your
Quest.

Yeah, about
that…

***Knowing Me
is the most important
thing in
Your Quest!***

The rest of it,
don't worry,
my Holy Spirit will teach you all you
need to know.

Sometimes you'll be reading in my
book, and something will really
speak to you.

Or you'll be talking to someone and
something they say just seems to
grab you.

You might have a dream,
or you may hear my voice speaking
right here in your heart.

I do all of this.

My Holy Spirit is doing these things
to communicate with you.

He's reading you Your Quest.

As you give your heart to me and let me guide your desires, I will fill you with desire to do my will.

You'll know through those desires what I really want you to do.

I have laid out
so many plans for you.

I have so many people I want you to meet.

You'll give to some;
you'll receive from some.

I want you to show up…

- at the right place
- at the right time
- with the right equipment
- …the right words,
- the right attitude,
- faith,
- and power.

My Holy Spirit will help you.

This will actually be quite fun and
very rewarding.

When times get tough,
just remember,
I am ALWAYS
with you.

I Am!

I love you child;
I will never let you go.

Lord, I love you!

Thank You
for coming into my life!

From The Book...

Hey Friend,

Did you make this your conversation?

Did you sense Jesus talking to you?

Did you give your life to Him?

If so, that was the best decision you could ever make.

Congratulations!

He referred to His Book, that's the Bible. So, I've gathered a few scriptures to get you started.

Taking time, reading His word, is time well-spent.

We're praying for you. You are now part of the most important Kingdom and family that exists, The Kingdom and family of God.

Keep The Conversation Going

Take some time with these scriptures, read them again and again. Circle or underline anything that seems to be meaningful to you.

God would like to continue this conversation with you after you're done reading this book.

We've added some pages at the end to get you started, but please get yourself a journal; paper or digital. Write down what you want to say to Him. Then listen for Him to speak. When you sense it, write it down. He loves you and wants you to continue to hear Him speak.

Like He said, there are many voices out there.

Trust Jesus to help you discern.

Scriptures (NLT)

2 Corinthians 5:17
This means that anyone who belongs to Christ has become a new person. The old life is gone; a new life has begun!

Isaiah 41:10
Don't be afraid, for I am with you. Don't be discouraged, for I am your God. I will strengthen you and help you. I will hold you up with my victorious right hand.

2 Corinthians 5:20
So we are Christ's ambassadors; God is making his appeal through us. We speak for Christ when we plead, "Come back to God!"

John 13:34
So now I am giving you a new commandment: Love each other. Just as I have loved you, you should love each other. "

Matthew 28:19
Therefore, go and make disciples of all the nations, baptizing them in the name of the Father and the Son and the Holy Spirit.

Matthew 28:20
Teach these new disciples to obey all the commands I have given you. And be sure of this: I am with you always, even to the end of the age."'

Acts 1:8
But you will receive power when the Holy Spirit comes upon you. And you will be my witnesses, telling people about me everywhere—in Jerusalem, throughout Judea, in Samaria, and to the ends of the earth." "

John 15:4
Remain in me, and I will remain in you. For a branch cannot produce fruit if it is severed from the vine, and you cannot be fruitful unless you remain in me.

John 15:5
"Yes, I am the vine; you are the branches. Those who remain in me, and I in them, will produce much fruit. For apart from me you can do nothing." "

Galatians 5:22
But the Holy Spirit produces this kind of fruit
in our lives: love, joy, peace, patience,
kindness, goodness, faithfulness,
23 gentleness, and self-control..."

Ephesians 2:10
For we are God's masterpiece. He has created
us anew in Christ Jesus, so we can do the
good things he planned for us long ago.

James 1:2
Dear brothers and sisters, when troubles of
any kind come your way, consider it an
opportunity for great joy.

James 1:5
If you need wisdom, ask our generous God,
and he will give it to you. He will not rebuke
you for asking.

1 Corinthians 10:13
The temptations in your life are no different
from what others experience. And God is
faithful. He will not allow the temptation to
be more than you can stand. When you are
tempted, he will show you a way out so that
you can endure.

1 John 1:9
But if we confess our sins to him, he is faithful and just to forgive us our sins and to cleanse us from all wickedness. "

Philippians 4:6
Don't worry about anything; instead, pray about everything. Tell God what you need, and thank him for all he has done.

Philippians 4:7
Then you will experience God's peace, which exceeds anything we can understand. His peace will guard your hearts and minds as you live in Christ Jesus."

James 4:6
..."God opposes the proud but gives grace to the humble."*

Hebrews 4:12
For the word of God is alive and powerful. It is sharper than the sharpest two-edged sword, cutting between soul and spirit, between joint and marrow. It exposes our innermost thoughts and desires.

Some Questions to Ask as You Read

As you are reading any chapter from the Bible, ask this question about these topics:

"What does this chapter teach me about...?":

- God
- The Father
- Jesus Christ
- The Holy Spirit
- The Devil
- Heaven
- Hell
- Prayer

- Family
- This world
- Forgiveness
- Sin
- My Future
- Me
- Work
- Money

Write your answers or thoughts in your journal. You'll be so glad you did.

Let Me Pray for You!

Heavenly Father,
I ask you to bless my new friend.
They've given you their heart.
They need healing in their life.
Lord,
I ask you to touch every area of their life,
especially guide their thoughts to think of
you so much more.
Over the next few days and weeks,
I ask you to begin speaking into their heart
and revealing your Word,
your will and Yourself to them.
Lord, they want to know You!
Show yourself powerfully to them!
In Jesus' name.
Amen!

Where Do I Start?

A great place to start reading the Bible is in the book of John.

Take your time. Maybe even lots of it.

Read the whole book of John all the way through. As you go, underline anything that seems to make sense to you or speaks to your heart. While you are reading invite the Holy Spirit to teach you.

Ask Him out loud...

"Holy Spirit reveal God's words to me.
Give me what I need to know.
Give me what I need to grow.
In Jesus' name."

Get One Thing Everyday

When I first started walking with Jesus, someone told me, "Joseph, if you just get one thing from God every day, you will grow." That has proven to be true in my life ever since.

I love to read God's Word until He shows me something. Get at least one thing from His Word every day.

When He speaks something to your heart write it in your journal. God's words transform us! The more attention we pay to them the more powerfully our lives are transformed.

It's Your Turn

We've added some pages here to get you started. Begin a conversation with God right now. Write down what you want to say to Him. Then listen for Him to speak. Be patient. Quiet your heart. When you sense a spontaneous blessed thought, write it down.

He loves you and wants you to continue to hear Him speak.

If you get stuck and say, "I don't hear anything!" Then answer this question: If God were speaking to me right now, what do you think He would be saying? Write that down.

Most people who've used this method have become convinced that it was Him speaking in those thoughts.

God is happy with you. He's glad you want to hear His voice. He loves you.

Enjoy this time with Him, I know He will.

Lord, speak to my heart!

_____

_____

_____

_____

_____

_____

_____

_____

_____

_____

_____

_____

_____

Speak, Lord, I'm listening!

_____

_____

_____

_____

_____

_____

_____

_____

_____

_____

_____

Talk to me Lord!

_____

_____

_____

_____

_____

_____

_____

_____

_____

_____

_____

_____

Lord, I'm listening for your voice.

Lord, I love when you talk to me.

_____

_____

_____

_____

_____

_____

_____

_____

_____

_____

_____

Lord, share some scriptures with me.

_____

_____

_____

_____

_____

_____

_____

_____

_____

_____

_____

_____

Lord, I love your voice.

Lord, you correct but never condemn.

_____

_____

_____

_____

_____

_____

_____

_____

_____

_____

_____

_____

Lord, here's what I'm thankful for:

_____

_____

_____

_____

_____

_____

_____

_____

_____

_____

_____

_____

More Information…

Prayer For New Life

If you could trade the life you've lived so far for the one God designed you for, would you do it?

If the Lord has been tugging at your heart to come closer to Him, it may be time to go ahead and give your whole life to Him.

If you've been weighed down with guilt and are tired of feeling ashamed and disgusted with how things have been going, it may be time! Time to finally say "yes" to a relationship, a real relationship with God.

He made a way for you to come to Him. He cleared a path. Jesus gave His life to cleanse you from all your sins and make you brand new. Are you ready?

The Bible says, "Everyone who calls on the name of the Lord will be saved" (Romans 10:13). Saved from what? Many things. The mess you're in, the future mess you're headed towards, especially Hell.

Give your life to Jesus and everything will become new for you. (2 Corinthians 5:17)

If you desire to have this new life in Christ, pray this now:

Heavenly Father,
I need you. I come to you as a sinner, needing a new life.
Forgive me of my sins. Make me brand new.
Give me a new life. Lord, I believe that you raised Jesus from the dead. Jesus, you are my Lord.
From this day on, God,
I belong to you. My whole life is yours. Let's live it together.
In Jesus' name, Amen!

Prayer For Power

It seems that Jesus had more power to live victorious than we Christians do. He always had the right answer that blew everybody away. He didn't seem to need to obey natural laws. He walked on water, raised the dead, healed the sick, and fed multitudes with a little boy's lunch.

Aren't we supposed to imitate Him? Aren't we supposed to try to be like Him? It seems foolish. It's kind of like a kid with a Superman cape that wants to jump off the roof of the garage. It's cute but definitely not effective.

There is a different way. Jesus said in Acts 1:8, "but you shall receive power when the Holy Ghost comes upon you". In 1 Corinthians 12, it says the Holy Spirit gives us gifts that are beyond human ability. In John chapters 14-16 Jesus introduces us to the ministry of the Holy Spirit through the most unlikely candidates– you and me! In the Book of Acts, the Holy Spirit came upon people who were praying, He came upon people when the disciples laid hands on them, but Jesus also promised that God would give the Holy Spirit to those who ask. Are you ready to ask? The only prerequisite is that you are a believer in Jesus Christ.

If you want to have power through the Holy Spirit, pray this now:

Heavenly Father,
I do believe in your Son, Jesus Christ. Jesus is my Lord. I want the same power that Jesus had so that I can imitate Him and live this life as He did. Lord, I ask you to fill me with your Holy Spirit right now. Holy Spirit, you are welcome in my life. Teach me. Lead me. Draw me closer and closer to God. Lord, use me to do whatever you want to do. In Jesus' name,
Amen!

Joseph Barlow

As the 10th of 14 children, Joe was born into a family that believed in training leaders and changing the world. Joe received his degree in Music Theory and Composition, after which he married his lovely wife, Nancy. Joe & Nancy have been married since 1985 and enjoy seven children and their families.

Being led by the Holy Spirit is the essential element of Joe's ministry and his daily life. Romans 8:14 says, "They that are led by the Spirit are Sons of God." The focus of Joe's life is to draw people to God.

His extensive business background has brought great strength to his ministry calling. Joe has literally been involved in the ministry since he was 11. Pastored for 16 years and a worship leader for over 30. He served as the Director of Living Word School of Ministry in Forest Park. He now runs Joseph Barlow Ministries where he focuses on writing books, writing and performing music, coaching, creating on-line classes, and ministry through social media.

His 20 plus years of corporate work include management for Tyndale House Publishers, Christianity Today, database programming, being a Microsoft Certified Trainer and the Chief Operating Officer of a $550 million hedge fund.

His children are making their mark in the world as well: Sarah Barlow is a world acclaimed photographer. Mark Barlow's music is available on all streaming services. Andrew, Natalie, and the rest are doing powerful things that we're sure you'll hear about in the future. (Isaiah 61:9)

Joe also has a side hustle playing guitar in restaurants with his 60s and 70s hits.

Joseph Barlow Ministries

Our Purpose
Friends, I started, JBM in October of 2008 knowing someday the Lord would direct me to it, but I didn't want to do it on my own. All in one day His direction came. He spoke to my heart saying, **"If you don't do this, there are many who will never be able to fulfill my will for their lives."** He also said, **"I have not called you to do this alone. You must have partners."** He assured me that He would send those who were called to be partners with me in this ministry.

JBM is financially supported by product sales and the generous support of our partners. If you believe you should join us, go to www.josephbarlow.com/partner.

Some of the ministries we've been fulfilling so far include:

Podcast: look for the Joseph Barlow podcast on any podcast service. Please, follow and leave us a 5-star review! ☺ That will encourage others to listen.

Missions Trips: so far, we've taught, sang and prophesied in:
- Costa Rica
- Honduras
- Portugal
- Luxembourg
- Germany
- Angola
- Liberia
- Uganda
- The Philippines
- India
- The United States

Who knows where the Lord might send us next?

Music: We've written and produced several albums and singles including:
- Faithful Is He
- A Day with Jesus
- A Longing Fulfilled
- Talk To Me Lord
- Healing Is Yours
- Know You

JBM Continued…

On-line Classes:
- Hearing the Voice of God & Journaling
- Wealth to the Nations
- Fresh Move: Living the Spirit Filled Life

On-line Ministry:
- Facebook group: "Daily Discipleship with Joe Barlow"
- YouTube
- TikTok
- Instagram

Books:
- Change is for the Brave
- Prayer Is…

Many more to come…

Traveling:
As called upon we travel and minister in churches with music, teaching, prophecy, and encouragement.

Coaching:
Both Joe and Nancy do personal, family and life coaching.

Local Meetings/Seminars:
Fresh Move meetings, Parenting Seminars, Empowering Ministers, and The Blessing

There's so much more to JBM. Please visit our website for more info and please join our email list.

www.josephbarlow.com

Let Us Know

How has this book impacted you? Let me know. Send me an email to share what happened while you read this book. This book is part of my quest. You can let me know through your testimony how I'm doing. It would mean a lot to me.

Send us an email:

myquest@josephbarlow.org

If someone gave you this book as a gift, please email them your story.

If you gifted this book to someone, write your email on this line for them.

Made in the USA
Monee, IL
10 July 2023